Check Your ASSETS & KNOW YOUR VALUE

A *Woman's Guide* to Becoming Her *Authentic Self*

KAREN ABBOTT-TRIMUEL

Check Your Assets & Know Your Value
A Woman's Guide to Becoming Her Authentic Self

Copyright © 2020 by Karen Lynn Trimuel

All rights reserved. No part of this book may be reproduced or transmitted in any manner, whatsoever, except in the case of brief quotations embodied in critical articles or reviews. This includes electronic or mechanical, photocopying, recording, or information storage and retrieval system.

For information contact:
KGT Live Productions, LLC
https://www.kgtliveproductions.com

Book Design By: Jose Pepito, Jr. ©
Collaborator & Editors: Victoria Thomas and Brenda Higgins

Library of Congress Cataloging-in-Publication

ISBN – 978-1-7362815-2-9 (paperback)

First Edition

This book is dedicated to you, the Reader.
Enjoy
Karen Abbott-Trimuel

TABLE OF CONTENTS

CHAPTER 1: A MINI INTRODUCTION 1
My Three-Year-Old Self..1

CHAPTER 2: KNOW YOUR VALUE..5
A Bible Story About Value 5
The Facts About Adam & Eve 7
A Look at Women's Search for Value..8
Final Thoughts on Adam & Eve 12
Reach the Goal: Know Your Value!...22

CHAPTER 3: GETTING BACK TO YOUR AUTHENTIC SELF..................23
A Fable About Pretense...24
The Inauthenticity of Women...25
A Personal Story About Finding My Authentic Self............................29
Reach the Goal: Be Authentic!..33

CHAPTER 4: DISCOVERING WHO YOU ARE..35
The Beginning of My Self Discovery 36
An Analogy of the Shepherd and the Sheep 37
The Lack of Self-Discovery Among Women..39
Reach the Goal: Start Discovering You!..42

CHAPTER 5: LOVING YOURSELF...45
Complete Transparency..45
Women Are Avoiding Self-Discovery 48
Reach the Goal: Start Loving Yourself!...50

CHAPTER 6: FORGIVENESS OF SELF 53
A Story of Self Forgiveness - Can You Be Kind to Yourself? 53
Women Forgive Last 55
Reach the Goal: Forgive! 57

CHAPTER 7: INVESTING IN YOURSELF 59
My Views on Investing in Self 59
Women Are Excellent Investors – Except in Themselves 62
Reach the Goal: Invest in Yourself! 66

CHAPTER 8: BUILD POSITIVE RELATIONSHIPS 67
A Story About Negative Company 67
How do you begin on this journey of positive relationships? 70
Reach the Goal: Build Positive Relationships! 77

CHAPTER 9: ROMANTIC PARTNERS 79
The Perfect Proposal 79
Women Follow Their Hearts and Not Their Heads 80
Reach the Goal: The Right Romantic Partner for You! 84

CHAPTER 10: MAKE A COMMITMENT TO YOURSELF 85
The Final Story Before the Curtain Drops – Self Inclusion 85
Becoming Committed – To Yourself 87
Reach the Goal: Commit to Yourself! 88

References 91
Acknowledgements 93
About the Author 95

Chapter 1
A MINI INTRODUCTION

My Three-Year-Old Self

I was three years old: A mature toddler of the garrulous, talkative kind.

If you have ever been a parent, there was probably a time when you wished you could give your three-year-old or preschooler away. Maybe temporarily, to get somewhat of a break.

Okay, maybe not literally. But do you remember those days, if you have experienced it with your little one, that they demonstrate the fullness of their 'terrible two-year-old' or 'terrible three-year-old' character, and you want to auction them off to the lowest bidder at that particular moment in time?

I think that would describe me to-a-Tee at that precise age.

I could walk and hold a conversation before I was a year old. You probably don't find that hard to believe today, if you know me in person, because of my flair for words and unbridled energy!

Maybe this is why my mother allowed me to play the game I am about to tell you now.

When I was three years old, my mom told me a story. I do not recall how or when it happened because…

I don't know. Maybe we remember less of our formative years in the moments when those significant events happen to us so that it falls on our parents to remember those pivotal moments – And store it in their treasure chest of memories that will be used during Storytime to us, when we grow up to understand the meaning behind the tale.

On this particular event that happened to my three-year-old self, I packed a handkerchief with my little three-year-old possessions, a handkerchief like Huckleberry Fin.

You may know of Huckleberry Finn – It is a book published around 1884 by Mark Twain, a story set along the Mississippi River, a satire on racism.

The character of the novel, Huckleberry Finn – Otherwise known as 'Huck' in the book – Usually packed his belongings in a handkerchief tied to the end of a stick when he was out and about on the road.

Well, this is exactly how I chose to pack some of my belongings on that particular day, my Mom told me.

I cannot tell you how I got the idea to behave like a Huckleberry Finn-like character, a character that represented the ridiculing of racism in 19th century America.

Maybe that will be a story for another time – If someone from my childhood would be so kind as to tell me.

Anyway, I digress.

I packed some of my belongings into a handkerchief on this fateful day and tied the handkerchief to the end of a stick.

I told my mom I was running away.

If you have ever had a two- or three-year-old around the house, you may understand the value of humoring your kid when they say or do certain flamboyant things - Sometimes.

Thus, you may not be surprised to note that my mom humored me and my little-handkerchief-on-a-stick.

She told me to go ahead. Runaway, kiddo.

Well – Dear Reader – I *did*.

I began to walk down the street - poor mother.

She had to follow me from behind, waiting for me to turn around.

I never looked back, and I kept walking.

Now, I know what you are probably thinking at this point. You are probably thinking – What kind of a mother was that? What did she do to her child that the little one would want to run away?

I would urge you at this point to take all blame away from my mother. She had nothing to do with the distinctive character that seemed to be taking me somewhere that no ordinary kid would usually venture.

To cut a long story short, my mom, still trailing close behind me throughout my runaway journey, stopped me by the time I got to the corner to cross the street and asked me:

"Where are you going, Karen?"

My response: *"I told you I'm running away."*

I was running away – Because I knew there was something out there that I needed to pursue. There was a goal that needed to be attained. And I was too impatient, even at age three, to start living it.

I didn't understand it then, but I understand it now. I was not running away from something or someone... I was running to something. I don't know what it was, but my three-year-old self knew there were great things ahead for me.

My mother tells this story often.

Thanks to her, I can tell the stories that follow in this book about the things I have begun to discover and the milestones that I need to accomplish as a woman. The milestones that need to be accomplished by *any* woman.

Perhaps – This book you are about to read today was a glimpse of what my three-year-old self saw, those several decades ago:

The enlightenment of the life of a woman and how she can discover her worth.

Chapter 2
KNOW YOUR VALUE

You Are Your Most Valuable Asset.

Valuable. Assets.

These two words have represented women since the beginning of time.

Whenever you've read about influential men in the history books, I can almost guarantee an influential woman was lurking in the background, lending her ideas, suggestions, and opinions to him.

A Bible Story About Value

Most have heard about the Biblical Adam and Eve.

Humor me for a while on this topic. You may or may not believe in Christianity or the Christian Bible - However, there is something to learn from this story if you would have an open mind to see how it could be a narration relating to your own life, and in fact, your value as a woman.

If you have not heard the Biblical story of Adam and Eve, I will narrate it now.

God created the Heavens and the Earth – The birds, the sea creatures, the land animals, the trees and vegetation – and so on. At the end of the work, God saw something was missing… God needed a guardian to tend to all that had been created. What better guardian could that be than *a man* to manage these affairs?

And so – God created Adam. The first man.

This is where the story gets interesting, though - I believe that from the first moment Adam was created, God already had a woman in mind as an extension to man's creation.

In dialogue, and treatises, and studies, there seems to be one common belief about the woman who was described to have been created out of Adam's rib: That she was 'the weaker sex' or 'the lesser person.' Or that she was solely created to take care of Adam, mere support and enhancement to his purpose.

As the story goes, Adam was in charge of giving all things their names, and he had dominion over them. Alright, let's call a spade a spade – He was the boss on Earth.

However – Even bosses get lonely. God saw loneliness consuming Adam and knew it was time to create his companion. The story goes that when God-realized man should not be alone, God caused Adam to fall into a deep sleep – And used one of Adam's ribs to fashion a woman, a creature that looked just like Adam – Only more beautiful looking, of course.

All women are beautiful in their unique and individual attributes.

In addition to her beauty, there were special characteristics and skills that she would embody when she was created, such as multi-tasking, organization, and finding a simpler way to complete tasks.

I would know this because these characteristics have been embedded in women as far back as the history books go.

As I mentioned at the beginning of this chapter, two words describe a woman: Valuable. Asset.

Therefore, why is it that in today's world, and, since the beginning of creation, certain blame has been ascribed to the female for 'things going wrong'?

The Facts About Adam & Eve

For some reason, a significant population of the planet blames Eve for man's downfall and, ultimately, humanity's problems. After all, if this meddling female had not eaten the forbidden fruit in the Garden of Eden where she lived with her husband Adam, humans would still be living in the Garden-like Paradise state today. Right?

In case you have not heard about the story of the Garden of Eden, I will tell it to you.

When God created man, Adam, and gave him dominion over all creation, Man was given a home on Earth – It was at a paradise-like Garden called Eden.

The Garden had everything a man could ever wish for: Natural interior decorating made up of the blooms of the Earth's earliest flowers, plants, and trees; four rivers that ran through the Garden, otherwise known as natural Jacuzzis; free food and drink in abundance that Adam never had to work for because the Garden was lush and plentiful in food that grew with no farming required.

Let's just say Adam was living it up.

The story describes God warning Adam about a tree that Adam was never to patronize in the Garden while living this paradise lifestyle. The tree was known as the Tree of Knowledge of Good and Evil. God warned Adam that he would die when he ate the fruit that grew on that tree.

Then, God created Eve, Adam's wife.

Eve ate the fruit from the Tree of Knowledge of Good and Evil after listening to some counsel from a strange creature in the Garden that she should not have heeded.

The creature told her that the fruit from the tree would make her wise if she ate it.

Maybe I should pause here to comment that as women, this may be one of our weaknesses. We are always looking for ways to improve ourselves because we think we are not good enough with the way we are. Can you guess what Eve was thinking? Do you mean if I eat this forbidden fruit, I will improve? I would become wiser?

Are you surprised by the rest of the story with Eve? Of course. She ate the forbidden fruit.

Damn.

You may be thinking: If I were Eve, I would not have eaten that forbidden fruit!

Before we start to cast stones at Eve, maybe there are some features that women today share with her? Maybe the same flaws still exist?

Let us consider Eve's flaws.

A Look at Women's Search for Value

Women Violating Laws of Nature for Self-Improvement.

Eve thinks: "If I eat the fruit, I will become like God? Would that not be an improved state for me?"

This was one flaw that made Eve commit the atrocity of eating something forbidden. She wanted to 'improve' herself.

You may argue that seeking self-improvement is not a flaw.

However – It is when it violates laws of nature. For the sake of argument, let us say that the law that God provided to Adam was a natural law that said: Do not eat the forbidden fruit, or else you will die.

Adam obeyed from the beginning. Eve did not. She was the first to fall for the potential that she could 'be better' than her current state. She did not seem to care that she would be disobeying a law to get there.

Women disobey laws of nature all the time to 'self-improve.'

I watched a documentary about a woman who thought she needed to have bigger breasts. She believed that it would be her form of self-improvement. She would look more beautiful and maybe attract more attention. She went for plastic surgery for breast augmentation. She had a negative reaction to the anesthesia. Unfortunately, she died and never got a chance to recover.

I am not condemning plastic surgery. However, if it's not broken, why try to fix it? The lady had perfectly normal breasts. What was broken that needed fixing?

Plastic surgery has been the saving grace for people who need it. For instance, it has given beauty back to burn or accident victims, women with breast cancer, or people who need corrective surgery on some organ, like their nose, to breathe better.

However – Surgery is an example of the violation of nature's laws for 'self-improvement.'

Self-improvement begins from within. A woman who is confident in herself from within would know how to look her best – Without challenging nature to get there.

This was Eve's sin. It continues to remain the sin of most women.

However, let us not forget one minute detail in this story of woe – God gave the instruction directly to Adam and not to Eve. Eve's attempt at self-improvement would have been isolated to a negative impact only to her if she had kept it to herself because the instruction had been for Adam. Adam's participation appeared to be required for their entire small society to go down.

Adam would likely have remained loyal to the instruction God had given him. Unfortunately, in women's attempts to self-improve, they usually take an incredible amount of society down with them.

It is what may rightly be called the 'cloning effect.' One woman who achieves 'self-improvement' through unnatural means is usually a role model for many more women to follow the same route.

To reiterate, this section is not to speak against plastic surgery. It is good when needed. However, it is an undeniable example to highlight other things that women do to 'self-improve' that negatively impact them and others around them.

Women Want to Be Like Someone Else.

This was Eve's second flaw. Adam was the ruler who had dominion over everything, except there was one thing that was forbidden – The tree of good and evil. They were not to eat from it.

As the story continues, Eve was convinced by a serpent – the strange creature in the Garden - that if she ate the fruit from the tree, she would not die but would become like God and would be made wise.

She wanted to be like someone else. I can't understand why it's so easy for us women to be convinced to do something we know is wrong because we think it will benefit us somehow, despite the consequences.

Have you ever seen a supermodel on a TV show, or observed a very lovely, or rich, or popular person at your school or place of work, or followed after some big influencer on social media and wished: Goodness! If only I could be her!

To become 'her,' you start to dress like her. And you start to make your hair like her. Or you even start to speak like her.

You cannot be someone else. Yet, women do it all the time. This was a flaw of Eve. It continues to be a flaw of women.

Women Need Collaborators To 'Do Evil' To Themselves.

We all know that Eve ate the fruit and nothing happened - Until Adam ate it with her. Maybe this is telling us something. Does failure require the collaboration of someone else? A man, another woman, a partner in crime?

I repeat – Nothing happened until Adam ate the fruit.

I remember the typical high school movies that I watched while growing up-the beautiful cheerleaders picking on the nerdy girl with big glasses. The school bullies, ganging up on a tiny boy and locking him up in the restroom after taking his lunch money. The college jocks, picking a fight with the Math Club members in a 'classy versus nerdy battle.'

Collaboration makes a society stronger. The reason why Eve's eating of the fruit was probably ineffective until Adam joined her was likely because when two (or more) agree as one, there is greater impact.

As women, there are many instances to indicate that we collaborate on more harmful things than good. Women are more notorious than men for lack of trust, backstabbing, and in-fighting, to name a couple of examples or three. As we are such emotional creatures (More so than men), we seem to thrive better as packs – For emotional support. Therefore, if there is a conflict, we want to gang up with our girlfriends, for instance, against the 'bad person' with who we feel conflicted.

Just like Eve.

Her eating the fruit and asking Adam to join her was a cry for emotional support. I have a notion that if Adam had been the one to eat the fruit first, he would probably have kept quiet about it and not sought 'emotional support.'

I think there may be witnesses reading this book that would testify to what I just described as a common trait of men.

Before continuing on the journey of women's flaws, it may be necessary to remind that this writing will not tear a woman down.

There is a saying: Discover the problem, and you have discovered the solution.

This book is a leisurely walk through some common problems we face as women – So that we can see the solutions to the problems together on these pages.

What else can we learn about women from Eve's features?

Final Thoughts on Adam & Eve

There seems to be one missing link in the tale of Adam and Eve. The narration of what happened when Adam and Eve were kicked out of the Garden. What arguments or what conversation would they have had with each other after they lost the garden? It is true today, as it would have been true, centuries ago, when Adam and Eve lived – Husbands and wives argue.

Eve ate the forbidden fruit. She told Adam about it, and Adam ate it too. God appeared and asked them what they had done.

Adam's response: *"The woman You gave me handed the fruit to me, and I ate it."*

Eve's response: *"The serpent deceived me, and I ate it!"*

(Talk about blame-shifting).

God's response: *"You are both banished from the Garden. Man, your reward for this act is that you will toil with hard work from this day. Woman, you will labor in childbirth from this day."*

God's position is like that of an employer. The employer may have rules around the workplace - For instance, stealing a coworkers' belongings at a workplace is not tolerated. Anyone caught stealing will be kicked out of the office or fired, pronto.

In essence, Adam and Eve were fired from their cozy jobs in the Garden because they disobeyed the employer's rules. I think God deserves some credit for trying to maintain order around the organization. After all, we make rules as humans to create order out of chaos in our own lives too.

Let us consider what became of Adam and Eve after God told them what to expect for disobeying the rules. We will call it "The Untold Story of Mankind's Getting Fired from the Garden of Eden."

What did Adam and Eve have to say to each other after they were asked to leave the Garden of Eden? The scene would represent the quintessential argument between a man and his wife, otherwise known as The First Argument.

The conversation probably went a little something like this:

Eve began by saying, *"Adam, you told me God gave you rules, but you didn't say our punishment would be like this if we ate of the tree of life."*

Adam may have replied, *"I told you that there would be consequences; you'd think that would be enough."*

Eve begins waving her finger back and forth, *"I'm going to endure labor pains while you work the land? That is all the punishment you get? Had God given me the instructions instead of you, we wouldn't be in this mess."*

Perhaps, after the argument, Adam asked God that if there were any life instructions that needed to be adhered to in the future, they should be given directly to Eve, too, instead of having him, Adam, as the intermediary.

Do you know how I know? Because after Eve experienced labor pains, we never heard about Adam or Eve getting into trouble after experiencing their punishments.

Perhaps this tells us something: If Eve has her instructions, if she is allowed to build her mind, and understand her value, that she is capable of being instructed directly, there would be more women who know their value and would not be making errors that rise to the magnitude of being kicked out of Gardens, out of Paradise, out of Opportunities, and anything else they hope to attain.

In other words - Eve should begin to realize that she is capable of following instructions about her life and doing something about it - Without waiting for someone else to do it for her, or second-guessing herself, or thinking she is incapable of attaining that 'something' unless someone validated her as a woman worthy of making those pursuits for her life.

How could Eve – or you - begin to harvest this worth about yourself? That you are worthy of whatever your heart dreams and desires?

You should realize certain things about yourself as a woman that make you worthy of pursuits that build you up, set you apart, and establish you as an individual who can become anything she wants to be out of life.

You are Influential as a woman.

So far, we have found out one thing about men, and one thing about women: A man gave up his leadership position because a woman demonstrated her inherent characteristic of influence when she persuaded the leader to do something along with her.

As a woman, your natural characteristic or tendency is influence. You can influence anybody and anything if you set your mind to it. After all, it seems evident that most of the influencers on social media are women.

The Playing Field Is Leveled.

It is often said that men make better wages or have a better status in our current society than women.

I believe that this saying has lingered for decades after women won the right to vote because women still believe that it is a factor that hinders them from becoming all they want to become.

However – This is not the case for the woman who knows her value.

Throughout my internal search and meditation process, I have come to find that two factors that we often hear are true, 1) you become what you believe, and 2) you attract what you believe.

If you believe that you are, and will remain lower-wage status, or second-class status, or on the wrong side of the tracks rank – You will always remain so.

If you believe that the playing field has been leveled and you can start to dare to do something like the well-known influencers of the world, it is possible. Even if you don't achieve affluence status as they have, you will achieve something in your little corner of the world because you believed.

I have had conversations with family members and friends throughout the years. I have discovered one thing amongst some of the female numbers of my conversation partners: They don't think they have what it takes to achieve 'XYZ,' whatever their 'XYZ' is.

I have watched women that I love and admire, doubting and second-guessing their dreams, goals, and aspirations.

The interesting thing is that they knew what they wanted to do at some point in their lives, but for some reason, their dreams never came to fruition because they were taken on another course. Why is that? Why did they allow derailment from the things they had aspired to achieve for themselves? I discovered why:

They have admitted that they didn't believe enough in themselves or trusted in their abilities to become those things they had dreamed of.

The result for them?

They decided to forego their hopes and park their dreams on a shelf and hide in the shadows of others. How did I come to know this? I came to know this because I believed the same things about myself. I didn't believe in myself or my potential. Now my newfound beliefs have led me to take my talents off the shelf, step into the forefront, and write this book you're reading now.

Come Out of The Shadows.

Let us talk about how women inherently live in the shadows, just because they are wives, mothers, or sisters.

We allow our zeal for others' achievements to be the reason for our living. If we have an ambitious, very career-oriented marriage partner, for instance, we would be there for them at company dinners, wait up for them when working late, clean up after them even though they're not pulling their weight around the house, or the family. And in the process, we neglect our own lives. We live in the shadow of them – or someone else.

It could be in the things we do for our children. There is nothing wrong with living for our children – But are we living for ourselves too? If the children have, for instance, some budding talent, we want to make sure that it is harvested well. We are chauffeurs to their ball games, ballet classes, and piano lessons – We help them with the homework and sports practices to ensure they are having all the stellar attention needed to become the best...

But in the meantime, what happened to our dreams as the woman who is raising that child?

We support our spouses and raise our children, and before we know it, the children are grown; our spouses are doing what they love, and we're in the background wondering what's next for us. That is the point where we have cornered ourselves into a place of, I don't know what is going to happen to me if, for instance, my husband passes. Or, I don't know what I will do with my life when, for instance, the children leave home to start living their own lives.

It is a bad feeling to be in a place of the unknown, to be lost in a world passing us by.

There is nothing wrong with the desire to be the best wife and mother that you can be. There is also nothing wrong with wanting to be a good homemaker for your family. If this is what you aspire to be in life, the bedrock that supports your family, while you cheerlead their lives, as long as you are happy and satisfied, that is very well done. It is also alright for you to stay in the shadows if you wish to be.

'Coming out of the shadows' is for women who feel incomplete, dissatisfied, and unhappy with where they are right now in life.

It is possible to be that woman who lives in the shadows, even if you are the CEO of a company and make six or seven figures.

It is possible to be that woman who lives in the shadows, as a homemaker who makes zero income.

Therefore, living in the shadows can happen to anyone, as it means you live because of others' interests and not pursuing your own true heart.

If you live in the shadows, others' lives will be the definition of yours. It leads to a deep-down feeling of voidness. You know something is missing from your life. It can happen to the CEO. It can happen to the homemaker.

It is time to come out and start to think, imagine, dream, and live the life that you want for yourself.

I heard another saying recently: Create the life you want by starting with a thought.

The things that we think are the things that materialize into existence.

If I think I will be one of the next astronauts who fly to the moon, my actions will start to take me in that direction as long as I believe it. I may need to have certain academic qualifications, such as a scientist. I would need to enroll in astronaut training and work hard to be selected. And so on. But my thoughts form my beliefs, and it begins to drive me towards the goal.

What have you believed about yourself that will take you to the life of your dreams because you are worth it?

Stop living in the past.

Continuing on the subject of things women need to do to realize their value, many are aware of the history of women and what they endured over the centuries: Unfair treatment, disrespectful behavior, abuse, and second-class citizenship status. Women did not have the right to vote until August 18, 1920, only 100 years ago, when the 19th Amendment to the United States Constitution passed in America. It was an indication of what society thought of us, and the backlash remains today.

The worst part of it is that we believed, accepted, and have embraced this treatment for centuries. This stands true in some countries today because of the culture, religious beliefs, and family history.

Women seem to have been taught, or at most, it is a part of the culture, that they take backseat status during this stage of their lives.

In societies where it is still the culture for women to be at the back – I pray that they too will experience the freedom that most of us have and can rise to the forefront with their presence being seen and their voices being heard.

However, in countries of the West where a woman can go to school like her male counterparts, where she can vote, and where she can do pretty much everything a man can do in the community, I do not believe there is as much of an excuse to say we have a lot holding us back.

If the women we most admire focused on what was holding them back rather than acting out their worth and discovering their destinies in the process, they would never have arrived where they did.

They represent a rising number of women who are no longer living in the past, which says: I can't because I am a woman.

Define Yourself.

Due to obsession with looks, competition with others, etc. women have had a major part in contributing to the creation of billion-dollar industries, such as cosmetic companies, plastic surgery, and apparel businesses all because as Eve demonstrated in our earlier example in this chapter: Trying to be someone that we are not.

As women, we have waxed, colored, pulled, tucked, and stretched in more ways that are beyond normal. We compete with each other based on size, looks, material wealth, etc. We demean each other, degrade each other, and gossip about each other to take positions that are popular with society's opinions, or, in the alternative, to hide our flaws by exploiting and revealing the flaws of someone else.

We are consumed and misguided by others' ideas and opinions, cultures, fads, world views, media, television, and anything else that influences us visually, emotionally, and physically.

If we continue down this path, we will become a clone society where everyone looks the same, dresses the same, and acts the same because we all want to look like the latest and trendiest people to experience our worth.

How boring.

We do this because we don't know our worth or the value of what we bring into this world as individuals with unique destinies and not cloned ones. Mistakes we make or have made in the past are often rooted in not knowing who we were or what we have to offer.

Let us use the world of music as an example. I have nothing against it. As a matter of fact, I love music and entertainment. However – Due to the hero-worship of music artists, as an example, I have heard of ladies who would go under the knife in a second to gain the backside, nose, or features of the artist they worship as their idols.

The problem is, we look to others to define who we are and what we do. Self-definition will develop you into the best version of yourself. You achieve it by listening to yourself and your circumstances – Not listening to the lives of others.

You ask yourself searching questions: What direction is life driving you toward now, considering your circumstances and the tools you have to work with, such as education, finances, or anything else that you could use to start making lemonade out of lemons?

This is how you begin to find yourself as a woman of value. What else can you do on this journey to discovering your self-worth?

The next point will take you deeper.

Dare to Dream.

The problem with not knowing who we are and what we want to do with our lives is because we do not give ourselves a chance to develop our dreams, goals, and aspirations. We allow others to take the chance for us.

Like that, we've allowed others to convince us that our purpose for 'being' is to tend to others' needs before taking care of ourselves. We have allowed people to talk us into doing things we don't want to do.

For instance, we can be so easily talked into new ideas because we don't seem grounded in our females' ideas! An example would be, being in a pleasing career. Still, because of someone else's idea that we move into another role or go in a different direction, we go along with the alternative views, then find ourselves doing something that we do not enjoy and become miserable because of it.

We go from knowing what we want to do for ourselves to do whatever others ask of us. Take a moment to think about the last time you did something that you wanted to do. You had an idea or set a goal and took a chance and trusted yourself.

How did that make you feel? Can you imagine where you would be now if you stayed on course and kept doing what made you happy? What would that look and feel like today if you had stayed the course?

How many times have you put your plan on hold to help someone else complete theirs? Well, it's time for you to get back on track.

Reach the Goal: Know Your Value!

Learn what it means to Know Your Value!

There is more to you than being someone's daughter, wife, and mother. You're more than someone's arm candy, baby machine, or happy homemaker. You have gifts and talents that only you possess, and that is immeasurable. There are some things that only you can do. There is so much more to you…a lot more. Knowing your value is knowing that you are uniquely and incredibly created, and for this reason alone, you should always be valued. Not dismissed, but valued.

You are the missing ingredient to making your dreams come true. Without you, it can't happen! Unfortunately, along the way, we've allowed our value to depreciate by allowing others to define our purpose, our usefulness, our future, and when released, our power.

Now, it's time to get it back!

Chapter 3
GETTING BACK TO YOUR AUTHENTIC SELF

Authenticity.

What does it mean to you?

I now know what it means to me. It means I have reached a point in my life – or at least, continuously working towards – where I know that I am validated. Confirmed. Confirmed as someone who knows her identity and does not need to switch sides, or be confused by other's opinions of me, or go begging for crumbs of recognition from other people's tables – Because I recognize myself as a worthy and valuable woman who knows her place in this world.

Let us talk about 'other people's tables' and why you should be eating only off your table for your life. It is part of the story I am about to narrate below.

A Fable About Pretense

I remember a concise tale made popular by an ancient Greek storyteller called Aesop. The storyteller lived about twenty-five hundred years ago.

It is the story of the jackdaw bird and the doves.

A jackdaw is a small gray-headed crow that typically nests in tall buildings and chimneys. The bird looks like a dove in body shape but does not have the same color of feathers as doves.

In this fable, the jackdaw birdie saw that the doves in a garden's dovecote were very well fed, receiving plenteous food supply, probably from the human owners of the dovecote, regularly.

The jackdaw wanted to live like the doves. She wanted to eat as well as they did! Therefore, she dyed her feathers white (as mentioned, her feathers were naturally gray) and went to join the doves in the dovecote, expecting to share in their food. And of course, she did - She had managed to look just like them so that the doves did not mind sharing their food with another dove - Or so they thought that was the jackdaw's identity.

The jackdaw managed to keep up the pretense of being a dove for a while, because after all, she had the body shape of a dove, and now that her feathers were dyed and painted white, she could pretend to be them as well!

We know that birds sound different when they make 'bird calls.' A sound the jackdaw makes when it opens its beak is not the same as what a dove makes. Therefore, so long as the jackdaw kept quiet, the doves thought she was another dove like them and accepted her.

Unfortunately, the jackdaw could not keep up the pretense forever. At some point, she forgot to keep quiet and let out a squawk, which did not sound like a dove at all!

The doves recognized that an imposter was among them, and of course, you cannot be comfortable having a stranger living with you who is pretending to be someone they are not! The doves did the respectable thing that they could think of - The doves pecked at the imposter with their beaks, the poor jackdaw, until she had to flee.

Unable to feed with the doves, the jackdaw went back to the park where her fellow jackdaws normally gather to feed. However, even her fellow jackdaws could not recognize her anymore because her feathers were painted white! They did not recognize her color or that she was one of them, so they kept her away from their food.

The jackdaw had nothing to eat at all at the end of the tale. Guess who ended up becoming hungry because of pretending to be someone she was not?

The Inauthenticity of Women

Pretense

The jackdaw's story shows that we must be content with our lot in life since being greedy is pointless and can even deprive us of the things that are ours. Creating a false representation and adopting roles that do not define you doesn't help; it merely hurts in the end.

Consider the jackdaw who pretended to be someone she was not. She had nowhere to go for food, the result - Perpetual hunger that hurts.

Ladies - There is nothing wrong with being a jackdaw if that is who you are. Don't paint yourself into a dove.

True – many people may think the dove looks nicer and maybe more colorful; and may even have more means for getting food if, for instance, human garden owners prefer to feed doves in their gardens than they feed jackdaws. This may mean the dove lives in a different class, and you, being a jackdaw, may want to pretend to be in that class to reap its benefits: For example, more food for the jackdaw for pretending to be a dove! In our case as humans or females, 'more food' may represent our pretending to have the means which we do not: Purchasing designer clothes, a bigger house we can't afford, a luxury car that makes us look good but makes the bank account look poor every month, etc.).

What's the result? Perpetual hunger, just like the pretending jackdaw who wanted to be a dove.

If you are not a dove - Don't pretend to be a dove. As a result, it will always be a jackdaw experience. Hunger.

In our modern world, the jackdaw's behavior represents women: Pretending to be people we are not because we think there is a benefit to pretending. The jackdaw thought she was benefiting by pretending to be a dove. She ended up getting kicked out of the food party. Plus, she also lost her friends, relationships, and other jackdaws she ate with because they could not recognize her anymore.

When I think of the jackdaw, I realize that I have also been guilty as charged in the past. I recognize that it is easy to fall back into the habit of pretending to be someone else.

It is unnatural to live in a false appearance. After all, your nature is different, and by silencing it or pretending it away, you are only decreasing yourself and stagnating your growth.

I have experienced this first hand because I was extremely insecure, indecisive, and had low self-esteem for a very long time.

Those characteristics were forged by the opinions and expectations placed upon me by others. At a very early age, we're often told how to act, what to do, who to be, and better yet… who we are. We are molded by our experiences at home, in school, in society, or in the workplace.

We define our viewpoints on beauty, perfection, and lifestyle through what we see on television. Television has become a big influence on all of us, especially when we are just getting to know ourselves and developing our personalities. We imitate and pretend to be what we see. We also look to embrace and accept our peer's validation as essential to who we are or who we become.

As I grew older, I noticed that I took on the personalities, looks, and opinions of people I came in contact with... family, friends, or colleagues. I took on the expectations of others instead of being the person I was created to be. As if I wasn't good enough, their opinions and suggestions were what was best for me.

It took a long time before I understood; the woman I saw in the mirror was a false representation of someone beautiful hidden deep and ready to be unveiled. I had been living according to everyone else's viewpoint.

The pretense is one area that robs us of our authenticity. What else could there be? I will talk about it next.

Past Experiences That Hurt or Scarred Us.

Some experiences hurt and leave scars, so you think the best solution is to pretend it never happened and hide it by becoming someone you are not. Why do you think the jackdaw pretended to be a dove? Could it be that she had experienced hunger at some point in life while living like a jackdaw, and the hunger experience scarred her? Could it be self-preservation, seeing that the doves had a seemingly endless supply of food; therefore, as long as she could be them, she would always have an endless supply of food?

If we have experienced something unpleasant in the past and are hurt by it, we tend to build protection around ourselves that hinders us. Just like the jackdaw who painted her feathers white, she became hindered from joining the dove's food party eventually; and even rejoining her community of jackdaws. The experience of hunger that she had endured while living as a jackdaw made her want to become a dove – And now, she had completely hindered her life because of that unpleasant experience.

Rise beyond your past. Do not let the scars hold you from your future. If, for instance, you wanted to be a nurse, and you failed the Board exams the first time – Do not let that scar keep you from trying again!

The previous times tried were not failures. They were merely discoveries of what does not work. Therefore, don't be scarred by them.

Another point could hinder a woman from seeking authenticity if she does not deal with it. I will mention it next.

Coming out of the Background.

Perhaps, sharing the moments when I realized that lack of authenticity was hurting me will help you on your journey to becoming your authentic self.

I no longer desired to be the false representation of myself and wanted to know the person inside fighting her way out.

She was no longer comfortable in the background of her own life. She didn't like what was being represented, and she could no longer sit back as she was being destroyed and knew she needed to surface if she was to enjoy a quality of life that was part of her destiny.

I know how challenging it is to break through barriers, structures, and chains that do not conform to who you are and how you want to live. It will be a fight for you to break away from the background and take your place at the forefront of your life unless you are comfortable with it.

That is why, in the war against taking your rightful position instead of the place that you have hidden for so long, you have to develop a new mindset: Get comfortable with being uncomfortable.

That's right – Uncomfortable becomes your new comfort zone.

You become uncomfortable when you are no longer satisfied with just getting by. You want to push the envelope. This is a big part of breaking away from a comfortable background and starting to discover your authenticity, which allows you to face the grit and uncomfortable things that placed you in the background in the first place.

A Personal Story About Finding My Authentic Self

Many years ago, I decided to become an executive assistant. It wasn't part of my original plans, and later I would discover that it would not be a career choice that would display my true talents and creativity. Discovering this truth about myself was very refreshing because the reason for this career choice had been out of desperation.

You see, I chose the path of being an assistant because my grandmother told me that as long as you knew how to type, you'll always have a job. She was a secretary herself, and little did she know that would become the greatest advice she could have ever given me because of circumstances that I would later find myself in.

At the age of seventeen, I would give birth to a baby girl and be challenged with the task of becoming an adult and caring for a child at a young age. Luckily for me, I was smart and skipped the 7th grade, graduating from high school at sixteen.

I attended a six-month secretarial course and was well on my way. This career choice would afford me the opportunity of supporting my family until my children were adults and had families of their own.

Something miraculous happened during the time I became an empty nester. I discovered that being an assistant was the field I chose because it was the quickest and easiest way to provide for my family. It wasn't my passion; it didn't display my creativity, nor did it fulfill me or make me happy. It was a resource that would provide for the survival I needed when I became a mother.

It was then that I had a symbolic birth, and my true self began to come alive. I lit up like a newborn, opening her eyes for the very first time as I saw a whole new world full of opportunities and possibilities before me.

Do not be afraid.

Even now, because of the unknown, I sometimes experience fear, anxiety, worry, and insecurities because I finally realized that I have been going through the motions of survival instead of living.

Now I am showing up and being transformed by making fear, anxiety, worry, and insecurity my step stools to elevate me to success. I am unveiling my authenticity and stepping up to the forefront of my own life. The one that was carved out solely for me from the very beginning.

I have discovered that I have to unleash my internal being, which is my authentic self, for me to be able to enjoy the rest of my life.

Dig Beneath the Surface of You.

I share all of this so that you, too, will find the heart to go deep and allow yourself to question what's really beneath the surface of who you are. When we pull back the layers and understand what worries us, excites us, or brings us joy, we will be able to find our truth and begin the journey that we came to fulfill throughout our lifetime.

Connect with your authentic self.

When we disconnect, we often find ourselves a million miles away and trapped by the afflictions, disease, and discomfort which cause depression, frustration, unhappiness, negative emotions, and inner emptiness. Kind of like a hole or void that we can't seem to fill.

All of this is a high price to pay for giving up our authentic selves to become a false representation that seeks to please others.

Discover your uniqueness.

Being authentic is simply discovering one's characteristics, skills, talents, and spirit. It's confident to stand firm in who you are in the skin that fits perfectly to you.

It is uncompromising when it comes to protecting yourself, knowing your value, and embracing all you have to offer this great big world.

Upon birth, you arrived as a unique and perfect creation. Unfortunately, once you were born and had a mind able to distinguish ideas, you were inundated with beliefs, cultures, opinions, and choices that would expose you to all manner of questions and confusion. You would ultimately encounter experiences that will dim your light and convince you to become someone you were not meant to be.

This is usually brought about by being dependent on others and usually lasts until you find your independence and are awakened internally and set on the path to restoring your authentic self.

Have a Re-Introduction to Yourself.

"Hello, my Gorgeous Self. Have we met? My name is (insert your name), and I am on a journey of being true to myself from this day forward."

Being reintroduced to yourself is one of the singular most important introductions you will ever have in this lifetime. The most important person in this world to you should be YOU.

You have to be in tune with yourself because you are created with everything needed to prepare you for or assist you through everything you would encounter in this lifetime.

You alone empower the strength, knowledge, and wisdom to overcome any experience. You have the intellect to know what to do, how to move when to move, and the direction you should move in.

The problem that most of us have found is that we've put our trust in others and have disconnected from trusting ourselves.

Get in-tune with your newly discovered self.

Once you are in tune with who you are, you will realize that there are many things required by a society that no longer fit the life you want for yourself.

Once you are truly aware that you are a unique creation, your life will take on a whole new meaning.

Permit yourself permission to freely choose your next moves.

Being your authentic self means being free to choose your path, breaking away from what was once considered normal, and releasing the chains that once bound you.

When you live in your true essence, your life is calm and peaceful; you experience happiness and empowerment.

On the other hand, if you display a false representation of yourself, your life becomes plagued with the fear of being exposed and rejected when the truth is revealed. Still, the truth of the matter is that rejection began the moment you rejected your true self.

Reach the Goal: Be Authentic!

Being yourself is the most beautiful discovery you can make because you live in the comfort of your own home (your skin), sharing gifts and characteristics with the world that are unique only to you, and making positive connections that will benefit you.

When being your authentic self, you raise your energy vibration, become committed to who you are and what your inner being dictates. You stop struggling with yourself and begin to embrace and enhance yourself.

When you know how you are in sync and plugged into your inner being, you know what's authentic or inauthentic by gauging your internal self's connection with your external self.

According to your true self, being authentic is speaking, deciding, and acting from your inner heart, not from external motivations.

When you know what is required of yourself and what is good for you, you know how to satisfy your internal needs by giving yourself positive aspects like love, understanding, and patience.

When you treat yourself well, what you say is in sync with your actions. This will allow you to make better decisions because you are in tune with yourself.

Learning to listen to your interior calms the mind and allows your authentic self to emerge. You are not living from a space of what others say or what is dictated by society.

Being authentic allows everything you decide, do, and say to be in harmony with who you are and what you stand for. This will bring about completeness with self, peace, and well-being.

Being authentic comes naturally and spontaneously when you love yourself because you know your worth and how valuable you are.

Authentic people set their values and act upon them. They have a consistent internal dialogue containing positive words of motivation, inspiration, reassurance, self-respect, and gratitude.

Love is key to all of this because you neither allow nor accept less than you know you deserve when you love yourself. Self-love allows you to shine from an authentic place because you know that you will be able to love others and become open to receive love by loving yourself.

Chapter 4
DISCOVERING WHO YOU ARE

The gift of life is about the discovery of oneself and not just about focusing on others.

You may recall this from the last chapter about authenticity. Discovery of yourself is the next level up after you have become your authentic self. This is what we will focus on in this chapter – Self-discovery.

Your authentic self is that person who is now occupying her valid place in this world, and not wondering whether she should look like that celebrity, or talk like that other person, or eat at that other person's 'table' by mingling with them because it will make her look good. She knows she looks good all by herself. When she has reached this authentic phase, then discovery begins —Discovery of all the pockets, facets, and outlets to express the real you.

Can you go back to when you were young, positive, determined, and knew exactly what you wanted to be? This was a time before everyone else got in your head with their opinions, ideas, and suggestions about who you are and was meant to be.

For most people, the moment they shared their dreams with others, those dreams were shattered by the naysayers because they didn't share the same vision. Naysayers would respond with "That's too big a dream!" or "That's nice, but you should think of something more attainable?"

Their negativity causes doubt, and your dreams began to fade. You do not revisit the idea because you think they are right.

Of course. What were you thinking! They were right to say you didn't have it in you to become a doctor! Or a top model. Or a beautician with your store at a prime downtown location.

It doesn't mean your dream disappeared. They are stored away and buried under the layers of what others think of you.

Now is the time for you to go to find a quiet place to rediscover who you are. A quiet place will allow you to hear and know your inner thoughts and tap into your personal feelings and emotions. There, you will find time to examine and acknowledge past experiences, mistakes, and choices, all of which will later become lessons that will lead you to future growth and awaken you to discovering the path that was originally set out for you to have a better tomorrow.

The Beginning of My Self Discovery

It was in 1993 when I watched a movie that would ultimately change my life for good. The movie was called Joy Luck Club.

By far, it is my favorite movie of all time because it was while watching this movie, I asked myself a question that would awaken hidden parts of me. The movie was about four Asian mothers' lives and their life lessons that would one day be shared with their daughters.

One part of the movie that I found myself repeatedly rewinding to make sure I heard the words the mother spoke correctly. It would be the first time I had ever heard these words spoken, and I found myself sitting quietly as I digested them.

The words of the mother to her daughter were, "You don't know your worth, and because you don't know your worth, you're willing to accept anything, even if it has no benefit for you."

Upon hearing these words, something inside me awakened and made me want to search my soul for answers.

The question I pondered over and over was: How do I learn my worth?

In other words, how do I discover myself?

An Analogy of the Shepherd and the Sheep

Some shepherds act as leaders: Guiding, nurturing, and protecting their sheep (followers). Then, some sheep act as followers who trust guidance, nurturing, and shepherd protection.

Some shepherds solely lookout for the wellbeing of those that trust them to keep them safe and out of harm's way. These are usually the shepherds that scope the land to ensure it has food for nourishment, room for growth, and a good atmosphere.

Then, some shepherds look to nurture as long as it meets their ultimate agenda. They are not concerned about the wellbeing of the sheep but merely about their selfish intentions and gain.

Unfortunately, the sheep are often naïve and trusting to their detriment because they are not in tune with the shepherd's character but what the shepherd can provide for them. They trust the one they believe controls their destiny and wellbeing. It's almost as if the shepherd becomes the god of the sheep. They solely rely on the shepherd for food, guidance, and protection. It wouldn't matter if the shepherd were leading them to the slaughter; the sheep wouldn't stray too far away as they are ok with relinquishing control to the shepherd because, at one period of time, the shepherd is trustworthy. Plus, most sheep are all following in the same direction, and it's easier to follow the masses.

It doesn't matter if the shepherd is taken off course; they are hardly ever challenged by their followers. We follow behind the ones that we view as having the power, authority, and control over the things we need, want, and desire. For the most part, we often put our self-worth, values, and beliefs to the side to not interrupt the authority of the one that we feel or FEAR have our destiny under their control. This is critical when thinking about self-discovery and what we've sacrificed or have agreed to sacrifice to become a part of a herd of followers.

However, there is hope for some sheep, as you will often find one or two sheep that are not following the others. It's either because something else has caught their attention or because they choose not to be a follower and have chosen to follow their own path. These are the ones that have discovered thinking for themselves and are curious to see what's on the other side for them. Although they may have strayed off – a good shepherd will go back and find them to ensure they are safe and assist them with joining the others on course to safety.

The other shepherd who only cares for themselves keeps moving along as he or she was never in tune with its herd in the first place.

What if sheep could discover themselves? If true, they follow a shepherd, but they also know boundaries and limits of who they are and their individuality so that if someone is leading them astray, they can recognize it quickly? Or, if they are leading themselves astray, they can know it before it is too late? This is the power of self-discovery. You know where you are going because you have discovered who you are. No one, not even a trusted shepherd, can misdirect you.

What does it take to discover yourself? Not having others defining who you are? What does it take to have boundaries that demonstrate that you have discovered who you are?

The Lack of Self-Discovery Among Women

Thinking You Don't Deserve A 'Self'

Knowing your value means knowing your importance and worth. Knowing you deserve to be valued. Unfortunately, some women I have met over the years do not 'know' that they deserve to be valued. They think others' value is above their own. Therefore, what is there to discover about themselves that is worth discovering?

Failure to Examine Your Life and Choices.

The key to discovering something is by studying it. Do you know that you are a masterpiece to be examined and studied? If you do not study yourself, you cannot discover yourself.

Therefore – Examine your life. Examine your choices.

For me, I decided to examine my life and my choices. To get to the answer, I was searching for, I would have to take a brave look at my past to find that little girl who once had all those bright ideas. I wanted to know why I didn't know my value or if I ever knew it? If I knew it, when did I lose it, and if something happened along the way to make me lose it, what was it?

My value began depreciating when others began to define my purpose, my usefulness, my future, and when I released my power.

I realized that culture, environments, experiences, and circumstances affect life and shape our future. Through this discovery journey, I realized that I lived most of my life just as the clown in the circus. I lived behind a smile when all along I was hurting and missing the most important person in my life.

I was missing me!

Pretending on The Outside Wastes Valuable Time.

When you live through your days by pretending on the outside to be happy or to be someone you are not, you are wasting valuable time that could have been spent in 'letting go' and allowing the real you to come out bit by bit.

I pretended with fake smiles and a false personality that did not feel like me for many years. On the outside, I'm sure people thought I had it all together, but on the inside, I was screaming and drowning in sorrow.

Though my face bore a huge smile on the outside most of the time, the inside told a much different story. Around others, I saw myself as the underdog or the smallest person in the room. I rated myself according to others' accomplishments and based their lives and experiences as being more valuable than mine.

Giving Without Receiving.

It has been said that 'it is more blessed to give than to receive.'

However, I will add a caveat to that nugget of wisdom: When there is a giving happening, there is always someone on the receiving end. It bothers me when you are absent from that end of receiving? Do you not think you deserve to receive too?

This was what happened to me for years. I would acknowledge the talents of others, and I would applaud them. I would participate in their growth. I gave a lot for their increase. Yet, I had no idea of the talents and skills that I possessed beneath my layers.

Even in relationships, I was the giver and chose people that brought no value to my life. I understood that every decision I made in the past was based on not knowing my value and accepting things even if they weren't good for me. I realized that I had given the best of me away to the worst of them. All because I saw everyone else as being more valuable than myself.

The question became: How do I go back to collect the pieces of me that I had given away so that I am made whole again? At that time, I had many questions, like Does knowing my value come because of what I've done, or is it defined by how other people view me?

How do you determine your worth, and where can you go to find it?

Failing to Understand That Discovery Is A Continuous, Life-Long Process.

As a unique, special, and exceptional woman, the beauty of you is that there is only one 'you' on the planet – And there are limitless things to discover about all the special things in you. This is why we are given lifetimes. Our lifetimes are intended for making lifelong discoveries. For instance, if you played a musical instrument in high school and think that is the end of your discovery and the things you can do, you are wrong. What happened to you in high school was one segment of your life. You still have a lifetime of discovery ahead of you.

This is why many women are grounded today. They discovered one thing about themselves. And they stayed there and did not continue to uncover more.

During the journey of discovering myself, which, as mentioned, is a continuous and never-ending search, I've come to the understanding that somewhere along the way, I lost myself in the translation by defining myself based on the viewpoint of others and by assuming the role of the caregiver as a priority over caring for myself. This was probably the reason why my self-discovery – or any attempts at it – was limited instead of continuous.

Reach the Goal: Start Discovering You!

Let me recommend finding the gold at the end of the rainbow to search for yourself and discover you.

Start with your character.

For instance, if someone calls you selfish - Don't get defensive. Take a journey down your life record and figure out if, more often than not, you are selfish - And why?

If you think you are compassionate, don't just stop at the thought. Consider examples of times when your heart had truly felt compassion for other people, and it was not just a public facade. Was it more often than not?

If you have been lauded as a leader, reminisce on what you have been able to do to lead. What are the features that make you such a leader?

Asking questions about the things you have been called or the things you have called yourself will help you validate whether those things are truly you – or not. It will help you discover the true you.

And if no one is speaking to you about who you are, or what they think about you: selfish, compassionate, leader, or whatever - Then you are not excused from making the discovery yourself. Self-discovery and making an effort at it will save you from believing that you are someone else.

More to be done than taking this dive into your characteristics, that is, who you are so that no one makes you into someone you are not. However - Start from here, and start discovering yourself!

Chapter 5
LOVING YOURSELF

Complete Transparency

I was born with pale skin, blue eyes, and sandy-colored hair. When I was born, my mother told me my father had doubts because I was so pale. I looked like a white baby instead of a black baby. As my mother put it, my dad rushed home, slicked back his hair, and came back to the hospital so that he could show more of a similarity to the baby that was just born.

I was born in July, and when we left the hospital, my dad wrapped me up in a blanket to hide my looks from the world. When my mother questioned my father, he remarked, "this baby looks white." Once my skin began to darken, and my eyes turned hazel, my father felt a lot better and was reassured that I belonged to him. Rightfully so, I had a lot of his features, like my big forehead and buck teeth. Well, I guess the teeth hadn't come in yet.

I remember asking my father about this story, and he said it was true. I also asked my grandmother which was my father's mother, and she said, "girl, you came out looking like a white child, and we had questions. You had sandy brown hair, blue eyes, and pale skin."

I was shocked – they both admitted to denying me within the first few weeks of my life.

The reason for my looks was because our genes are amazing! My mother's mother had a white father and a black mother. My grandmother had hazel-colored eyes, pale skin, and the only difference was that her hair was black. Other than black hair, a lot of her features carried over to me.

That's not the part that I'm transparent about. I just wanted to share that little tidbit of information to let you know how other people think and the chaos my birth caused.

We come into this world not caring about or knowing any flaws about ourselves. We are completely ok with how we look, act, feel, and, most importantly, who we are. It is not until we're engrossed with others' opinions of what's wrong with us or what could be better that we began to change the views that we have of ourselves.

From a very young age, people have always commented and complimented the color of my eyes. At first, I didn't understand why because we all had eyes, and they came in an array of colors. As a child, I didn't think of myself as any better or any less than anyone else. I felt beautiful, smart, and I thought I knew everything, or as much as a child could know. I was talkative, a little bossy, but very helpful at times. I loved people, and I wanted a lot of friends. I thought the entire world was beautiful, just like me.

It wasn't until I started kindergarten that I learned that I wasn't perfect and had flaws in my looks. This is where I learned the difference between beautiful and ugly. Who was acceptable or unacceptable? The people you played with and the stigma you would receive if you went against the grain. I was only five years old, and for the first time, I was being introduced to the pressures of fitting in, being accepted, and/or rejected.

Let me tell you; kids can be the cruelest!

In kindergarten, I learned that I had a big forehead for the first time, and because of this, I was made fun of daily. Next, the boys in the class would continually rate us, girls, as pretty or not. You have to ask yourself, where did those little children learn such toxic behavior. Thank goodness I was considered pretty, but my forehead held me back from being considered the prettiest.

Most parents won't admit it, but their children reflect them: their ways, beliefs, views, and behaviors.

At five years old, I began to view myself as defective and not pretty. The confidence I had in who I was and the beauty I possessed was shattered at five years. The funny part of all of this is that I had the same forehead as my father. I also had the same forehead as my siblings. The foreheads never came up in our family because we didn't see it as a problem. We didn't see it as a problem, but the world saw it as one, and for years to come, I would be reminded of how big my forehead was in most settings that I would be a part of.

Every day, when my mother combed my hair, I asked her to give me a bang to cover my forehead. From the age of five until my late thirties, I wore either a bang or swoop across my forehead to hide what I considered to be my defect. It wasn't until I looked in the mirror one day and saw what that little girl saw before she became layered with others' opinions and views. I discovered my beauty and love for myself. For the first time, I saw my defect as an enhancement that holds all the talents and gifts God gave me for storytelling.

I now say that I needed a bigger skeleton to hold the brain that God equipped me with, to hold all the information I would need to share with the world. I no longer need to wear a bang, or my hair swooped across my forehead. I have a forehead like my father, and now that he has passed away, I'm more than proud to wear it as a jewel in my crown.

That is the power of self-discovery.

There are certain harms that women are doing to themselves by denying themselves the journey through self-discovery. They deny themselves of this journey for various reasons. I will talk about those reasons next.

Women Are Avoiding Self-Discovery

Self-Hate Cannot Lead to Self-Love.

If I had hindered my development with self-hate because of the opinions of: I had a big forehead, or I was not 'rated' as the prettiest by the boys at school, I wonder where I would be today?

Would I have done something about my forehead, maybe surgery? Maybe, I would have been too ashamed of my features? Would I have ever realized that my features are a crown, and they represent my ancestry, my father, which is me?

The result of my accepting myself was a journey that took me to love myself for who I was.

Women are guilty of self-hate, and it hinders self-discovery.

Women Sit on The Fence About Loving Themselves.

"Do I look pretty in this dress?"

I have seen that scene in movies several times. A woman, asking her spouse whether the outfit she is wearing for the day looks good on her.

If the other person, the spouse in this example, responds according to their mood during that day. Perhaps, angry, vindictive, or any other negative emotion, does it mean you will not love yourself or the way you look because someone felt like saying they don't like your dress? How do you think you look? That's what matters.

When you have self-discovered yourself, and therefore, have come to love the person you discovered, you will, for instance, know the type of clothes or fashion that suits you to the optimum; and which appropriately accentuates your physical assets. Or, as another example, when you love yourself, you would not fall to pieces if someone criticized your looks or your work.

Therefore, as a result of self-discovery, you would not remain in the school of – Am I awesome, or am I not? I don't know!

You would have come to realize that you are, in fact, awesome.

What about you? Are you one of those women sitting on the fence and watching women who self-love, but don't have the guts to love themselves?

Women Lack the Boldness to Come Out of Comfort Zones.

It requires boldness to love what others do not. To accept yourself when others do not.

What is this phenomenon called 'boldness'?

Boldness means not being afraid of taking risks and being innovative.

You would never have guessed that being bold involves being innovative, which means doing something new, would you?

The concept of doing something different from what we have been used to is why many would remain in the comfort zone that does not get them up to arrive at a self-love destination.

If you can't do something new, how will you innovate? And if you can't innovate (Do something new), how will discoveries of the things you love about yourself happen to you?

Maybe it is time we stopped sitting behind the fence and stuck with watching women who are daring to love who they are, making it in life, and enjoying life.

Maybe we need to stop getting stumped by someone else's idea of how to love ourselves and be bold enough to do it.

Reach the Goal: Start Loving Yourself!

There are a few things I discovered along the path to loving myself. Let me share them with you now:

Loving yourself begins with getting to know who you truly are and accepting and embracing that person.

It's also acknowledging your strengths and weaknesses and being willing to make the necessary enhancements and adjustments to become a better you. Oftentimes we become like sponges and soak up the views of others. It's best to find out what you like and dislike and trust your own opinions. Spend some time alone writing down your thoughts and feelings.

Instead of storing them away, take the time to go back and read them. We spend time with people we want to build relationships with; why not spend quality time with ourselves. Learn to appreciate what you have to offer to yourself.

Loving yourself means exploring new things about yourself.

Step out of your comfort zone and try things that you've never tried before. During my discovery period, I began writing poetry, which ultimately led to writing, directing, and producing theatrical productions. I recently became an author due to converting one of my plays into a novel, "Ladies Night Unmasked," and authoring the current book you're reading right now. Through the exploration of self, I have been able to add the title of author to my list of accomplishments. If you had asked me what my talents were before I began my discovery journey, I wouldn't have been able to find my voice to put it into words.

One of the greatest things you can do for yourself is to find your voice and allow it to be heard. Don't dumb down to make someone else feel good about themselves. This should go for every aspect of your life.

The person who always agrees and takes on others' opinions is often silenced for another person's voice to be heard. When you speak up for yourself, doors will open. Don't allow others to put words in your mouth, mean what you say, and say what you mean.

It is fine to agree to disagree at times, and if people can't respect your opinion or your voice, beware of those people. Stop being afraid of doing what you know you are capable of doing. Part of loving yourself is taking up for yourself and allowing yourself to be the person you are meant to be. We protect what we love.

You owe it to yourself to fulfill your dreams and live your passions. When you have a passion for something, you have a strong emotional connection to it. Have you ever watched how a musician holds and plays their instrument?

It is as if they become one, and that's because the instrument's energy and the person are strongly connected. What we hear connects us emotionally because we are drawn to the mutually connected vibration of the artist with the instrument. The passion of the artist is heard and felt through the instrument, which ultimately becomes beautiful music.

If something brings you happiness and you're not harming yourself or anyone else, then go for it and enjoy it. Explore everything about yourself that you possibly can.

Love yourself and embrace your gifts and talents. They are a part of who you are.

When I write a script and create a production, something inside of me is awakened, and I go into this internal spiritual place that is unexplainable. It feels so good because I've done something that no one else can deny me of.

I've created something original and unique only to me, and no one can take that away or dispute it.

Find what excites you, explore it, and enhance it. Please bring it to life and watch your spirit come to life as well.

Loving yourself means spending time to build and encourage yourself.

Stop looking for others to validate your accomplishments. An accomplishment is something achieved successfully, which means it is already validated.

Loving yourself means focusing on the positives instead of the negatives.

It's so easy to look at what's not working instead of building on what is. Celebrate the small things and take time to pamper yourself. It can be as little as treating yourself to an ice cream cone, taking a walk in the park, or enjoying a spa day. Read a book (Ladies Night Unmasked), spend time with people that uplift and encourage you, and don't forget to dance. Dancing is so liberating and freeing. Allow your body to move to the beat, against the beat, or whatever your heart desires.

Just move!

It will take you in the direction of self-love.

Chapter 6
FORGIVENESS OF SELF

A Story of Self Forgiveness - Can You Be Kind to Yourself?

Forgiveness of self is tough to do when you've been bombarded with guilt, shame, and embarrassment. Especially when you are young and impressionable. When I was seventeen, I gave birth to a beautiful baby girl.

Giving birth, a time in which a husband and wife often celebrates, for me was a lonely experience. Many people looked down upon me during my pregnancy, like I had leprosy. Though I had my parents and siblings in my corner, the world was ruthless. I spent many years trying to prove to the world that I am a good person. Yet, I couldn't forgive myself for the burden I put on my mother, the struggle I endured as a single parent, or the looks and comments I received.

Because I couldn't see myself as valuable, I was never kind to myself. I didn't give myself a chance to be the best that I could be. I saw everyone else as more valuable than I was, and I treated them better than I treated myself. It was as if I was lucky that they were even spending time with me.

When my daughter was a teenager, I remember coming home from work, and she was waiting for me at the door. She hurried me into the house, snatched off my coat, and asked me to sit down beside my son as they had something exciting to show to me. As I sat down, she inserted a video into the recorder. It displayed various pictures of me scrolling across the screen as it began to the most beautiful music.

I felt a tear run down my cheek, and at that very moment, I no longer carried the shame of that teenager. I knew my children were the greatest blessings that God could have ever bestowed upon me. My daughter and son were the two people I loved most in this world, and they loved me unconditionally. I know they came into this world at the very moment they were supposed to. They were birthed through my womb and would later serve as great contributors and assets to my life. It was then that my children helped me recognize my value. I will forever cherish them for choosing me as their vehicle into this great big world. From that day forward, I lifted my head like a proud mother of two exceptional children.

As women, we are harder on ourselves, unforgiving of our shortcomings, often thinking of ourselves as average, not special, never giving ourselves credit for what we've already accomplished, devaluing our worth, and unworthy of self-forgiveness.

I want to take some moments to talk about the features that women have in common, which makes us unforgivable.

Women Forgive Last

Understand That Past Regrets Dictate Future Actions.

Be sure to know that along the journey to knowing your value; the past will always show its ugly head in the present to haunt you: Something that you did in the past, something you were unable to achieve, stands in the way of you being nice to yourself because of past mistakes, errors, or experiences!

If you don't face the past, it will try to pull you down every chance it gets and bring you right back to your starting point.

If You Keep It A Secret, You Cannot Be Free from It.

Secrets are a beast!

They are worse than any physical disease because, most of the time, they are the root and cause of most physical diseases that we encounter. Instead of killing your flesh, they kill your soul, and the only way to stop it is to release the secrets.

When we think of releasing a secret, we think we have to tell it to someone, but we also have other options. One way that helps me is by writing it down and getting it out.

Please put it in an envelope and write released on the envelope.

For me, I release the past, pain, and secrets by writing them out in this way. You should then burn it, shred it, or destroy it in some way. The point is to get it out.

Another way is to talk to a therapist or a life coach – Hopefully a neutral and impartial party.

Be sure you don't share your secrets with people that will throw it back up in your face when they are mad, or your relationship has ended.

The final thing you need to do to release a secret, mistake, bad choice, or whatever you want to call it is to forgive yourself or the person that caused it.

When you release the secret, you release yourself from it.

Forgiving Others Includes Forgiving Yourself.

We often talk about forgiving others but rarely do we forgive ourselves. How can you forgive and release others and never release or ease your pain? You have to love and forgive yourself for everything else to fall into place.

Forgiving others is simply you loving yourself enough to free yourself from the power of their actions.

Forgiving yourself is acknowledging what you've done and admitting that you're apt to make mistakes and are not perfect; only then are you released from regret and prepared not repeat the offense or actions. When your soul connects to your ask or act of forgiveness, it can be set free.

Every time something surfaces from your past, take a moment to acknowledge what it is and say "(insert your name), I forgive you" and then add my favorite word, "Next!"

I always say next because I am well aware that something else is sure to follow. I'm not going to kid you; if you're anything like me, you know many mistakes made in the past will resurface to be forgiven. Only then can you be free.

Don't Permit Guilt Tripping from Others.

Once you forgive yourself, don't allow others to hold you to past mistakes. If your mistakes have affected the lives of others, ask them to forgive you as well. If they give you their forgiveness, that's a great thing, and if they don't, you will still survive because your heart was sincere in the ask.

Either way, you'll need to keep moving and never look back; or that thing will jump right back on you and slow you down.

Always remember to release others because we all have been offended or have offended in one way or another.

Remember when we forgive others, we're saying, I know who I am, and I do not accept your actions towards me. I do not accept it, and I will not allow that to enter my energy or my spirit. I forgive you, and I'm releasing it and letting it go.

Reach the Goal: Forgive!

When we forgive ourselves, we're saying: I love myself enough to acknowledge the hurt and pain that I've caused myself and/or others. I know that if I acknowledge what I've done, deal with it, I can let it go and not repeat the actions against myself or others. I've learned my lesson, and through forgiveness, I will pass this test.

Forgive, Release, Let Go, and Be Free!

Chapter 7
INVESTING IN YOURSELF

My Views on Investing in Self

Investing in yourself takes constant sacrifice, deposits, and risks to gain a return on your investments. The greatest reward is to grow your self-worth and confidence. We often talk about and look for the greatest financial investments. But we forget those investments that may not be financial but are priceless and just as valuable, if not more valuable, and offer us the greatest returns.

Other Types of Investments to Consider:

TRUST – Trusting in oneself and the choices that you make is key. Trusting the process states that you believe everything will work in your favor, and you choose not to operate out of fear. Trust allows you the freedom to view things from a positive point of view. It also opens you up to endless possibilities as you began to look at things from different angles. You're trusting that you've given your all to ensure you have a successful outcome. Better yet, KNOW, it! Trust and doubt work against each other, so be sure you're not straggling the fence. If you trust, there can be no doubt, and if there's doubt, please know that trust is nowhere in sight.

TALENTS – Acknowledge the value your talents provide as they are an extremely critical source for enhancing your life. Every person has a talent. Rather it has been discovered or yet to be discovered; it is most certainly there. There is a wise saying, your gifts (talents) will make room for you. That is if you use them wisely. There was once a bartering system in place where people made exchanges for things they needed or wanted. They provided a service, exchanged items, etc., based upon their skills as money was yet to be created. Believe it or not, some people still use this system for survival. Take the time to find out what your talents are – they can enhance your life. Plus, you never know when or if a bartering system will return soon with what we've experienced in the past years.

LOVE – Put your love behind your passion and watch it grow. We invest our time and energy in that which we love. Self-love fuels the soul, contributes to our growth, brings about happiness, enhances our lives, and builds our confidence. Where there is love you will find true commitment and loyalty. Love invested correctly has the greatest return because it's the greatest of all investments you can make into yourself.

TIME – This is a precious commodity. It's often not respected and mostly neglected. If you respect time, it will respect you, and you'll find that you'll have more of it to complete the necessary tasks at hand. They say time waits for no one, but it does move with the momentum of those that recognize its value.

PATIENCE – It is a virtue that is to be commended when one exemplifies it. Patience refines, enhances, and improves. It also allows you to be in tune with time. It prepares you to be in a position to receive the goods when it's time to come your way. Good things come to those who wait or to those that are patient.

WEALTH – Understanding the true meaning of wealth is significant. One of the most important forms of wealth is GOOD HEALTH. Our health consists of our minds, bodies, and spirits. We must take care of our health by providing proper nourishment, getting the appropriate rest, and being aware of our physical, mental, and spiritual well-being. Investing in your health is a major contributor to your happiness, peace of mind, and longevity of life. Without it, everything is ultimately thrown off course, and you find yourself unable to meet goals, live your dreams, and flourish in life.

Investments aren't just financial – though there are many books to help you plan for your future, if none of the investments mentioned above are in place, you can never fully reap a complete return on your investment and enjoy all that life has in store for you.

Therefore, investing in yourself is investing in wealth of a better kind than mere money.

At this point, I would like to highlight those things that women do that rob them of self-investment. I will focus on this in the next section.

Women Are Excellent Investors – Except in Themselves

We have gone down the rabbit hole in this book: You read about how women neglect their well-being for the benefit of others; how the wife will sacrifice her life goals or career to see her spouse achieve theirs; how the mother takes the backseat to raise her children and watches life pass her by; how the woman in the office knows there is more to her than that job she has held for years, but she does not think she is worth going higher or doing what she is most passionate about….and so on.

The bottom line and summary of many of the subjects we have touched on in this book are: Women invest in others – But often, not in themselves.

As a woman, how do you invest in yourself? Let us count the ways.

Indulge!

Indulge yourself in the things that make your life more pleasant.

Always remember to be good to yourself and do things for yourself that make you happy. Investing in yourself yields the greatest return on your investment. Why? Because you benefit the most from it.

When you're happy and doing well, everyone that you care for reaps the benefits from it.

Live in the Now.

Put your money where your life is and find ways to enhance it.

We often talk about investing and saving for our retirement. It's a great thing to plan for your future, but what about your life right now? Many people may never make it to retirement. I'm not telling you not to invest in your future.

I am saying, don't forget to invest in your moments as they are happening right now. Tomorrow is not promised, and every day should be a day to be grateful and a celebration of being on the upside of the ground. So why not invest in both – what do you have to lose?

Enhance Your Life with Self-Improvement.

Are you increasing in your wisdom, knowledge, and understanding of how things work in the world around you? Are you investing in the enhancements of your gifts and skills by reading, researching, taking classes, learning a new hobby, sport, or instrument?

Remember always to put something to the side, do something you enjoy, and make an investment in the most priceless and profitable source, which is you.

Spend time and energy making your life better.

Steal away some quality time for yourself every once in a while. Find a place to shut the noise out and listen to your inner thoughts or bask in the silence.

Get in tune with your breath, feel the beats of your heart, listen to your body as it speaks to you with all of the quirky sounds that it makes.

Appreciate Yourself.

Take some time to look in the mirror and see the beauty that is staring back at you. Learn to admire and embrace that person. You're unique, and there is only one you, and you'll never find any duplicates.

You might see people that look like you in your family, but I can guarantee that their personality doesn't completely match yours.

Think about your next move and what needs to be done to make things happen in your life.

Take some time just for yourself, and don't feel guilty about it or allow anyone else to make you feel guilty.

Do Not Compare Yourself with Others.

Make enhancements – not drastic changes. Stop measuring yourself by what you see in others.

Just because someone is smaller than you or larger than you, or their hair is longer, shorter, curlier, or straighter, their body is shaped differently. Their features are more enhanced. None of that means you have to change you to match them because you feel like they are more appealing or receiving more attention than you.

When we change ourselves based on others, what that says to the world is, I'm not happy with myself, and I'm not good enough based on the ideas and ideology of one tiny section of society.

It never works, and you're never going to be happy in the end. Remember, 'self' always knows the truth even if others are buying the lie.

Be Health Conscious.

Take care of your health because there is only one you. Women are natural nurturers of everyone except themselves.

We will make sure everyone around us has what they need, and we will neglect ourselves during the process. We will make sure all doctors' appointments are kept and reschedule ours in a blink of an eye if someone or something else requires our attention.

We'll work ourselves to death, run our children to every appointment or activity they have, and we'll see to the needs of our spouses, family members, and our friends.

We'll clean the house, cook the food, and everything else that comes up throughout the day, but when it comes to taking care of ourselves, we'll push ourselves off and move to the back burner until there is time…which is hardly ever.

We'll go and go and go and go until our body breakdown, and we have no choice but to pay attention.

By that time, we're usually hit with some serious health matter because we didn't notice the signs, alerts, bells, and whistles to slow down.

The top three killers of women are heart disease, cancer, and stroke. I always call them the stress diseases, and there is no wonder why they are the top three killers of women.

We are the most stressed people on earth. We take on so much, and we never let anything go. We've fought and continue to fight for equal rights and to be given the same chances as men.

We forget to fight for men to take on some of the responsibilities that we've been doing for years.

We've taken on more and haven't released anything to make room for it. We're asking for more and piling it on, and we're so busy trying to prove we can handle it, but our bodies can't handle it and are crashing. Our brains are burning out as well.

Women, it's essential to have an annual physical. It's also important to raise your hand and ask for help. When you're feeling overwhelmed, take a moment for yourself. It's okay to say no, turn some things down, and let go. The problem with us is that we're so used to tolerating pain that we don't turn our attention to ourselves until it's too late.

Reach the Goal: Invest in Yourself!

You are very important, and you have been the glue that has kept most things together. Just know that if you're no longer here, the wheel will continue to turn. It may not turn as smoothly as it did when you were a part of it, but it will still turn.

It's alright to take a break, and most importantly, it's always okay to take time for yourself.

If you don't, you may not be here to see the fruits of your labor, which are your successes and advancements through life, the growth of your family, and time with future generations.

You might not see the success of your dreams fulfilled. You will be missed, but please know the world will still go on without you.

Therefore, invest in you, and let the world realize the gem they have living in its midst!

Chapter 8
BUILD POSITIVE RELATIONSHIPS

A Story About Negative Company

Bad friends will destroy you or at least try to...

I know this topic very well as I experienced an incident with someone that I considered to be a friend who shook me to my core. I worked for a company decades ago, and I was the senior assistant.

My colleague and I had become good friends, or at least I thought we were friends. Let's give her an alias, and we'll call her Lucy. At that time, I was a single parent of two children, and I worked hard and sacrificed daily to provide for them.

One day, Lucy invited my friends and me out for drinks with her and her friends at a nightclub in her part of town. The following Saturday, we all met up and had a great time. We laughed, drank, and partied hard.

As I arrived at work that following Monday, I noticed no people around, which was strange because all of the offices were empty, and Lucy was usually at her desk before me. Then I was approached by my manager and asked to join her in the conference room. When I walked into the room, I noticed that the company's president and all the executives were present. I thought to myself, this is strange. Did I miss the memo inviting me to this very critical meeting?

They all sat around the table with very severe looks on their faces. The president motioned for me to sit down, and as I took a seat, I noticed Lucy – my friend sitting across the table from me, crying. When I asked if she was ok – I was sternly asked not to speak to her at any time.

The first thought that came to mind was if we were being laid off. Then came the bombshell. I was informed that my colleague had reported that I brought a gun to work and threatened her with it. Before I could get a word out to defend myself, I was bombarded with people shouting at me with disrespectful words in a very demeaning way. I couldn't get a word in at all. I was alone and the only black woman sitting in a room full of white men and women. I felt defenseless. There were only three black people in the entire company. I had been subjected to all types of racial jokes, unfair treatment, and disregard for me as a person in the past. I took it because I was a young single mother with small children to provide for. But this…I did not deserve. I was horrified, devastated, and hurt by what I was hearing. I was called names, the things that were said…I can't say them here – it's just too much to bear and relive. But I feel I must go on because even though I wish it were not true and would have been a dream, it wasn't.

They had Lucy share her story, and I couldn't believe what was coming out of her mouth. She said I approached her, opened my purse, brandished a gun, and told her to meet me in the stairwell. She stated that I told her that I would use the gun if she didn't do whatever I told her. She was to do all of my work and never tell a soul. She was so afraid that she did exactly as I had requested.

I looked Lucy in her eyes, and I asked, "why" I never owned a gun, never held a gun; a matter of fact, I have always been deathly afraid of guns. Again, the room abruptly began to get loud with racial slurs, disrespectful names, and threats regarding my livelihood. Finally, it was my turn to speak, but before I was allowed to say a word, the president said, "We should call the police and have you arrested." All I thought about was my two children. What would happen to them, and who would raise them. This couldn't be happening to me. I pinched myself, thinking I would wake up from this nightmare, but I was still there. Sitting in a room with monsters. I gained my composure, and I asked Lucy: When did this happen?

She stated that it had happened several weeks before but that she was afraid to tell. My next question was, "if this happened, why did you invite my friends and me out dancing with you and your friends?" She immediately denied it and said that we had not been out and she didn't know what I was talking about.

I asked if I could make a phone call from the phone in the room and put it on speaker. They agreed, and I called one of my friends, let's call her Shirley. Once Shirley answered the phone and was made aware it was me, she asked me to tell Lucy she had a great time on Saturday and we must do it again soon because it was so much fun.

Shirley mentioned Lucy's name several times during the call and stated they exchanged numbers, and she'll be sure to keep in touch. When I hung up the phone, the leaders began to apologize profusely because they realized that they had been lied to. Lucy finally admitted she was lying and said she was sorry. She stated that our manager put her up to it, and she didn't want to do it. The manager denied it, and no one believed her because of what had just happened.

They told Lucy that it was unfortunate, but they had to let her go because of her actions. She got her belongings and left. I was asked to return to my desk. Can you believe that? I was shaken and devastated.

She didn't have to go through the scrutiny or ridicule that I did, nor was she mistreated or disrespected like I was. There was no mention of calling the police. She was just politely told that, unfortunately, they had to let her go. The saddest part, she had to be planning and plotting for a long time while pretending to be my friend. That's not the most painful part; what if she would have been successful with her plan. What then? It wouldn't be long before they would find a reason to lay me off, and I didn't fight it.

Unfortunately, there are all types of opportunists in this world, and some will do almost anything to ensure they make it to the top or reach their goals. I wish I could say that was the last time I experienced such behavior, but I can't. It might not have been to that extent, but it has happened. That experience taught me to always be prepared and to CYA. If you don't know what CYA means, it's simple – Cover Your **ASSETS!**

How do you begin on this journey of positive relationships?

Surround Yourself with The Right People.

Part of knowing your worth is making sure that along the way, you build a winning team. You are worthy of being surrounded by people that have your best interest at heart. The deposits determine part of your success from those that surround you. Do not be mistaken; not everyone in your circle is rooting for you to win. You must pay attention to those you consider as your friends. Be open to embracing other cultures and ages, as your team should always be diverse. There is absolutely nothing wrong if all your friends don't look like you. Diversity is good, and we can learn something new from each other.

Positive relationships are those relationships where deposits and withdrawals are being made simultaneously.

Education and information should be streaming between you at all times; if you're surrounding yourself with people who do not make positive contributions and enhancements to your life, turn and walk away quickly. There should always be growth in all relationships.

Positive growth.

Know Your Human Enhancers & Detractors.

Every day, we will encounter and interact with people of all types. There will be some that will leave a lasting positive effect and influence on your life, as well as those that will bring negative energy that can throw your life off course if you're not paying close attention.

I call the positive people 'enhancers' and the negative ones 'detractors.' For you to reach your full potential, both will play an important part in your life.

Enhancers are people that bring greater value to you, your life, and your experiences. They are people that recognize your potential and take a personal interest in helping you grow and become successful in your endeavors. They can become your secret weapon and are usually your silent cheerleaders.

They often stand in the background cheering you on while seeking opportunities to introduce you to people and things that are usually beneficial to your life. One of the downsides to some considered to be enhancers is that as you grow, eventually, there will be less of a need for them in your life.

Once you begin to move on, there can be some resentment because they are no longer a part of your growth and development.

And there is no longer a need for them to be recognized for their contributions.

Enhancers benefit from you as well. That's right, and there is an exchange that flows between the two of you. As long as they are a part of your circle, they reap the benefits of your good fortune, just as you did from theirs. They have made a major investment in you, and some may reap a return on their investment, some may increase their growth and development just as you have yours, and some receive fulfillment just by releasing deposits in you.

Remember, they connect to people and places that will help you get to exactly where you want to go. It's something about the energy that ignites from you that makes them take a greater interest in you.

Enhancers are usually people that have not forgotten the contributions that others have made in their lives. They are people that have made a conscious decision to pass it forward and invest in others.

It's much easier to sponsor and support someone or something you believe in.

Only good things can happen when you connect with a positive enhancer. Positive + Positive = More Positive.

When this happens, there's a deposit and withdrawal that the two of you experience simultaneously during your relationship. These positive connections are usually seen in good marriages where couples work together to build happy memories or experiences and successful business relationships where business partnerships are created and thrive.

As well as friendships that are successful, empowered, and unbreakable.

You Need People That Will Help You Bring Out the Fullest Version of You.

By ourselves, as humans or individuals, we have a purpose. Still, we need the connection, energy, and investment of others in a positive way to assist in bringing our purpose, talents, and gifts to fulfillment.

No one can honestly tell you that they got where they are all by themselves. There has been some level of the positive influence that encouraged and motivated their lives.

Alone, we can only fulfill a part of the purpose of our existence, but when connected to the right people, we can explore, share, and build on the purpose for which we were created for.

This is why we tap into and connect with positive people (sockets). We have to be plugged into the right sockets for our positive energy to flow to allow their energy to become a charge into our lives and ignite and/or help us enhance our abilities.

Understand the Law of 'Plugging In'

Every successful person in this world made a connection with someone who influenced their life and played an important role in becoming a success.

When you were a child, a family member, teacher or friend saw something in you that piqued their interest, and at some point, they chose to take time to teach, support, or influence your potential. There was a deposit of some sort placed in your life through them.

Let me give you an example: An electronic device that is never plugged in or charged doesn't have the energy to fulfill the purpose for which it was created. An outlet socket that never has anything plugged into it can never release its energy, thus also cannot fulfill the purpose in which it was created. It is only when the two are merged that each can fulfill its purpose.

A deposit and withdrawal are happening simultaneously, and the two receive an equal benefit. I have one more example. You purchase a beautiful lamp, and the reason for its creation is for two purposes:

1) its beauty; and

2) to provide light in dark spaces.

If it is never plugged into the socket, it will never give off light, and it will only fulfill half of its purpose. You can see its beauty during the day, but its beauty will fade in the darkness when it is dark.

When you connect the lamp to the socket, the socket can release energy into the lamp, and the lamp can fulfill its full purpose. It then becomes a beautiful lamp whose beauty has been enhanced by the light that it gives off, especially in the darkness.

Without your enhancers, people can see you, but your greatness and beauty will only fade in others' backgrounds if you're not connected to the right sockets. Do you want to be someone who stands out in a crowd or someone that gets lost in the background?

Enhancers Help You to Reach Your Goal.

An enhancer can help you build upon your potential, and before you know it, you've reached your goal a lot faster than you would have by yourself.

Have you ever heard someone say, "I could have never imagined my life being this good?" That's because what they imagined for themselves was only based on what they could do independently. They never took into account what they could do with the help of others.

A Note about Detractors.

Detractors are negative people that take away from your quality, character, value, and reputation. They see you, study you, and then latch on to you to suck the life out of you. They are very clever, and if you're not alert, you won't see them coming.

You'll look up one day and wonder where they came from. They are usually very cunning, like the wolf in Little Red Riding Hood or like Lucy. It wasn't until Red Riding Hood came closer before she could see the teeth on the wolf that was disguised as her grandmother.

It is usually not until we get bitten before we recognize someone who is a detractor.

Features of a Detractor – They Give Wrong Ideas for Your Life.

Detractors are usually people that have the greatest ideas about what you should be doing with your life. The unfortunate part is that they never line up with what you want to do with your life.

Detractors are also people that try to live their dreams and goals through you. They are often too lazy to do what it takes for themselves, but they hang around and benefit from all the good things that come your way.

They have great ideas but no resources or the potential to see them through. They always have excuses for the condition of their own lives and are always willing to make you feel bad about your misfortunes as well.

Beware of the Fault Finders – Another Feature of Detractors.

Detractors are the people that find fault in everything you do and are the quickest to ruin a good mood.

They are very negative people that walk around with a cloud hanging over their heads.

They discourage you from doing anything that would be of benefit to you. They are quick to smile in your face and stab you in your back just as quick as you turn around. They seek to destroy all the positive relationships that took years for you to build.

Detractors are Reputation Killers.

When given a chance, a detractor will destroy your reputation and decrease your value in the eyes of others. They will take your words and intentions and turn them on you.

They will creep into the cracks of your life like water and tear it apart at the seams. This is true for both romantic relationships, family relationships, and friendships.

It's easier to manipulate and control you if they have you all to themselves.

Detractors Believe in You – To Your Detriment.

The interesting thing about detractors is that they believe you have great potential. Their job is to make you believe you don't because misery loves company.

If you tap into your potential, you may begin to see them for what they truly are - Bloodsuckers draining the life out of you.

Detractors are Haters.

Detractors are also known as haters because they hate to see you succeed. They try to throw every obstacle in your path to stop you from reaching your goal. They can be a spouse or someone you love that verbally abuses you, a manager on your job that does everything within their power to stop you from being promoted to the next level, or a so-called friend that has done everything possible to discredit what you've said or done.

Beware of those you consider to be your friends.

A friend is someone that favors or positively promotes you. We often have very few friends but many acquaintances. An acquaintance is someone who knows you but is not quite a friend.

I believe about eighty-five percent of the people you will contact within your life will be acquaintances. They know you, but they are not trying to be connected to you in any way. Not all are detractors, and some can be enhancers in some ways without even knowing it.

Use Detractors as Your Motivation to Rise!

There is a positive side to detractors. Once you realize you've been duped, they can become your greatest motivators. You will desire to move so far away from them that it will set a fire in you that will inspire you to excel.

Also, they are a source of motivation for you to prove them wrong. Whatever they did to detour you, you will eventually use that fuel as motivation, thus becoming somewhat of an enhancer.

Reach the Goal: Build Positive Relationships!

When you can learn to decipher between the enhancers and detractors in your life, you will move in the direction of being surrounded more by enhancers to increase your value.

Remember - The goal is always to know your value and find more ways to increase it. Therefore, go out there and build positive relationships that will increase you!

Chapter 9
ROMANTIC PARTNERS

The Perfect Proposal

I can remember as if it was yesterday…when my husband proposed. He invited me over for Valentines' dinner, and it was the most thought out, loving, and delicious spread that I had ever seen. I entered through the kitchen and noticed he set the table like restaurants, complete with doilies and everything. There were also a dozen red roses in the center of the table. We ate steak, baked potato, salad and drank delicious wine. Then he escorted me to the living room. As I entered the living room, there were valentine decorations, a dozen pink roses, and chocolate-covered fruit, along with a bottle of chilled champagne sitting on the table.

I can't tell you what else was there because I couldn't see through the tears. I was in awe by the attention to detail, which showed me just how much he cared. Then he said, "I don't have a ring right now because I wasn't planning on proposing, but I can't see my life without you, and it feels right. If you want me to wait until I get a ring, I will." I immediately said, "no, you can tie a string around my finger – I'll marry you." It has been almost eighteen of the most amazing and loving years. The best lesson I can say that I've learned in our relationship is that if we put the work in and focus on our marriage, everything else will fall into place.

This is the perfect Segway into what we should discuss next in this book about you and your value- Having a romantic relationship that respects and is worthy of you.

Women Follow Their Hearts and Not Their Heads

Remove the Blinders.

Everyone wants to be loved, to experience love, and to give love. The only problem is that most of the time, we enter into romantic relationships with blinders.

We're led mostly by visual or superficial aspects instead of listening to our instincts. We enter into relationships accompanied with our self-esteem and worthiness intact. Before we know it, we can become so smitten by the other person that we drop our guard and decrease our value to assist with increasing theirs.

Our inner being alerts us to a very uncomfortable feeling when something isn't right; rather, it is a person, a situation, or being in a certain environment. Just like animals, we can sense danger, feel the need to be still, walk away, or move on. Trust your instincts. They will never lead you astray.

Many women often dream of their perfect proposals and dream weddings. They often invest more time and effort in the wedding than actually thinking about the type of person they choose to marry or the marriage itself.

The dream is more about the fantasy than the actual reality. It's understandable because as young girls, we grow up with the animated Disney stories and characters feeding us nothing but happily-ever-after stories without sharing what happens in between the kiss and the wedding.

Invest Time in Knowing the Other Person.

Take your time and get to know the person. Make sure you have something in common with them. Always remember that you can't change anyone but yourself.

If you see red flags, acknowledge them and don't think you can fix them. Remember everything and everybody isn't for you.

Most people have been fooled by looks, charm, words, and material things. In the end, people that were led down the path of deception are often left with far less than they began with - if anything at all.

Do Background Checks, Also Known As 'Ask Around'

Take your time to listen and decipher what's being said and why the person is saying it.

Find out all there is to be known about this person that wants to spend time with you. Learn about their family, their beliefs, their livelihood.

Do your research and pay attention, so you don't have to pay the price later down the line.

See how this person fits into your life. How do they interact with your family and friends? Are they attentive to your needs, or is the focus all on them? These are all questions that need to be answered and answered honestly.

Remember that You Are Already Complete.

In the movie '*Jerry McGuire,*' the actor says to the woman that he discovers he can't live without "You Complete Me." At first, I thought that was the most romantic thing I've ever heard until I began to discover who I was and the power I had within.

What I have discovered is that we should never look for someone that completes us. We're already complete, and we're already whole. We can join with someone who can enhance who we already are, but they can't complete us.

If a person 'completes you' during your relationship, when the relationship is over, and they walk away, they will be walking away with that part of you that 'they completed.'

You'll find yourself looking for someone else to complete you again because you'll never feel whole or complete because you gave that part of you away. You released control of part of yourself to someone else.

Have A Partner That Values You.

Make sure that you are valued in your relationship. Never allow someone to devalue you to add value to themselves. If this is the case, you are merely in the relationship to stroke their ego, which will, unfortunately, be your sole purpose if you carry on with such an unhealthy relationship.

You'll never receive any benefits from a relationship like this. It's one-sided, and there will never be room for a second ego because your partner's ego is big enough for the two of you.

If You are Giving, and Nothing is Being Given Back, Move On.

Relationships are 'give and take,' and no one should have to bend until they break to prove their love for someone else. If you're not receiving any positive, beneficial factors, then it's time for you to move on.

If you stay, you will find yourself shrinking until you disappear. What I mean by disappearing is you won't even recognize yourself anymore.

Sharing your life with someone you love and that loves you should be a beautiful experience.

It should be ever forming, growing, and building. Life, fulfillment, and enjoyment doesn't stop because you decided to settle down with someone in a committed relationship. There should still be laughter, love, and companionship.

Don't Be A Wallflower – Voice Your Concerns.

If you're in a relationship and don't like how you're being treated, speak up. You should be more concerned about your pain than if someone else is feeling good.

If you are in a situation where you feel you can't speak up, then that's a tell-tell sign that you shouldn't be in that relationship.

You have to protect your physical, mental, emotional, and spiritual state at all times. Every relationship that you encounter should be a healthy one. If not, this would be a good time to use my favorite word – Next!

Reach the Goal: The Right Romantic Partner for You!

Remember, you're not the property of anyone. You are here to experience and live your life during this lifetime however you choose to live it. With that choice comes the ability to choose whomever you wish to share your life with, so make sure you choose wisely.

My grandmother once told me, "You never want to be a 'should have, would have, could have' woman." I was only twelve when she told me that. I didn't know what it meant then, but I know what it means now. It means you don't want to look back over your life when you're older and have regrets. You want to be able to look back and be happy with the choices you've made and know that the choices were beneficial to you.

As we become older, we'll find that there are more years behind us than in front of us, and we won't have any time to catch up.

Therefore – Don't waste your days on time-wasting relationships.

Chapter 10
MAKE A COMMITMENT TO YOURSELF

The Final Story Before the Curtain Drops – Self Inclusion

We live in a commitment-phobic world. It is amazing how reticent individuals can be to make commitments even to themselves! People tend to be merely 'involved' in their own lives. They do not commit to making their destinies!

To many, life is a surface engagement that does not take them deep into the richness of self-discovery, or building self-confidence or, overcoming obstacles. The surface is comfortable. There is 'no need' to get so 'aggressive' about making a difference in their own life.

Frankly, that is what the 'involvement versus commitment' attitude provides.

What I've learned from my career as an assistant to leaders is that it takes a lot of commitment to ensure they are completely supported. I am not just 'involved' in work. I must be committed to it.

I have worked for some awesome leaders who took the time to reciprocate the commitment it takes to have a successful business relationship throughout my career. Those leaders would go over and beyond the call of duty to ensure that I found time to have somewhat of a work-life balance or as much as possible.

We had mutual respect, admiration, and support for the value we each brought to the working relationship and our partnerships. In business, dependent upon who you work for – you can often find yourself on the giving end for a majority of the time and hardly on the receiving end.

So, depending on where you land, you often find yourself in various working relationships – some being successful and positive and others being unsuccessful and negative.

I've worked for leaders where I felt like a valued partner, and on the other hand, I've also worked for people where I felt like I was their slave. Their wish was my every command. It was clear that I was there to supply all of their needs and relinquish and neglect mine. You're probably saying this sounds like the Shepherd and the Sheep analogy? It totally is!

I was an assistant for more than thirty years, and I'm grateful for the skills and opportunities I received because they allowed me to provide for my family.

I can truly say that I have seen a lot throughout my career, experienced a lot, and have met some incredible people…both positive and negative. I'm still in contact with those leaders (shepherds) who were concerned about their employees (sheep) and displayed it through their leadership. But for some, I pray that one day they'll look back and seek forgiveness for their treatment of others and realize that people are more important than things, power, and selfish wealth and gain.

I believe that Karma is a person having to experience the hurt, pain, or discomfort they have put on others. One thing is for sure Universal Karma surfaces at its appropriate time.

It took decades for me to realize I chose a role that required me to give more commitment, focus, and concern to someone else than myself for a majority of the hours of the day. The only time that I could truly care for and think about myself or my needs was in the late hours of the night, and that's when I wrote most of my writings.

I'm not saying that being an assistant is not a good role to have. I am saying that it took many years for me to realize that it was no longer the role for me. Secretly, I was bursting at the seams on the inside as my creativity and passions were being ignored by me. In my role of taking care of someone else, I wasn't allowed room for me to invest, trust, or commit to myself. It took total commitment away from me, and I realized that there wouldn't be much of me left if something didn't change. You know what they say: If you don't use it (talents), you'll eventually lose it. Or you might miss the open door when it's time for you to walk through it.

How do you enter this place of commitment to yourself?

Becoming Committed – To Yourself

Enter a Formal Agreement with You.

It's time to commit yourself. A formal agreement that, once you come into the knowledge of who you are and knowing your value, as this book has been teaching, you won't ever forget as you have taken all necessary steps mentioned in this book to arrive at this end goal - Commitment.

It will take will, desire, and constant action to be successful in knowing your value, and over time, you will be able to measure how successful you have become by the changes that will show up in your life. You will see your value as your authentic, creative, unique self develops, and others will see and experience it as well.

If You Can Commit to Others, You Can Do the Same for Yourself.

We're comfortable keeping commitments to others. That's easy!

This is when you'll commit to examining yourself so that sleeping beauty can surface and live her fullest potential. It's time for you to show up in your own life and start taking your rightful place – unapologetically.

Self-Commitment Will Start to Unearth Your Hidden Treasures.

This is easier said than done because it will take practice. We have been operating the same old way for years, and now we're trying something new. You will be exposed to the true you and all the choices you've made over the years, good, bad, or indifferent. Stay the course because there is a diamond hidden deep that you will treasure for the remainder of your lifetime.

Reach the Goal: Commit to Yourself!

As long as we are on this road of discovering who we are and acknowledging the value we bring, doubts will arise. It's alright to have doubts, but acknowledge them and keep on moving. It's time for you to show up in the equation related to your life, and sticking to your commitment will allow the greatest person that has ever been hidden to arise... You! – Your life is your most valuable ASSET!!! Check your assets, know your value, and become your authentic self.

REFERENCES

Aesop's Fables

Aesop's Fables (Date unknown). *The Jackdaw and the Doves*.

ACKNOWLEDGEMENTS

Thanks to my loving husband, children, and grandchildren for their support motivation, encouragement, and continued support.

Thanks to my amazing mother for her support and the stories shared in this book of my childhood.

Thanks to all of my family, friends, and supporters for your encouragement.

I hope you have found the information shared in this book to be helpful. My heartfelt desire is to use my life experiences as examples to empower and encourage others as they embark on their journeys of becoming their authentic selves.

ABOUT THE AUTHOR

Since childhood, Karen has always been passionate about writing and storytelling. Born and raised in the suburbs of Chicago, IL, her biggest dream was to perform on stage for thousands of people one day. But unfortunately, the plan was delayed a bit.

After attending Taylor Business School, she worked as an assistant for various c-suite executives of fortune 500 companies for over 30 years. As the years would continue, she never forgot her passion. Her inspirations come from real-life situations and creative imagination. Her goal is to make people laugh, think about life choices and make positive changes. She's using her platform to inspire, motivate, encourage and offer solutions. Karen has been writing for over three decades, with her first stage performance in January 2000 entitled "Hear Our Cries Lord." She has established an outstanding reputation for writing quality entertainment. She has written, directed, and produced a host of stage plays, including "Ladies Night Unmasked" (recently released as a novel). Karen's motto, "If I can positively touch one life, my life's purpose will never be in vain." Get ready world, Karen has a host of motivating, inspiring, and encouraging stories on the way to change the world!

For Speaking Engagements or to Connect with Karen:

>Website: www.kgtliveproductions.com
>Twitter: @KatzStories
>LinkedIn: Karen Abbott-Trimuel
>Facebook: KGT Live Productions

ALSO WRITTEN BY
Karen Abbott-Trimuel

Ladies Night Unmasked

SIGN UP FOR OUR NEWSLETTER

Be the first to learn about Karen Abbott-Trimuel's new releases and receive exclusive content!
WWW.KGTLIVEPRODUCTIONS.COM

www.ingramcontent.com/pod-product-compliance
Lightning Source LLC
Chambersburg PA
CBHW020912080526
44589CB00011B/563